MANDOLIN

DEAD MAN'S TUNING

VOL. 1: BASICS

BY: WILLY MINNIX

To My Sweet Cousin,

I hope you enjoy reading this book

as much as I enjoyed writing it,

without you it wouldn't exist.

Mandolin: Dead Man's Tuning Vol. 1

Chapters

INTRODUCTION

Hello, my name is Willy Minnix, and I am looking forward to teaching you how to play mandolin. The method that I am teaching you is an alternate method using a cross tuning known as Dead Man's Tuning or DDAD tuning. I have found that playing in this tuning is a rewarding and fun way to learn the mandolin quickly. It allows me to immerse my students into the exciting world of the mandolin very quickly, and the paybacks are instant as people realize that they too can make music when they initially thought they had no hope of ever playing.

I am a firm believer that music is the language of the soul, and it is my goal and heart's desire to be able to help give a voice to your soul, so that you can in turn add that voice to the great chorus of voices that have gone on before.

I hope you have a blast learning and playing your mandolin!

God bless,

Willy Minnix
Richmond, IN
2011

CHAPTER 1: THE MANDOLIN

If you are reading this book, I assume that you either play mandolin already in what is commonly referred to as Standard Tuning, or you are new to the mandolin and want to learn how to play. Either way you are in luck. If you are a seasoned player, this book is the first volume of a series that is an in-depth look at a tuning that I believe has not been explored to its full potential. Included in addition to the three types of tunings covered are several tabs of old and new songs written especially for this tuning, songs that have been arranged for this tuning, and even a few songs arranged for playing with standard and Dead Man's Tuning, as well as chords, picking patterns and a great deal of other information that will help you really develop in this style.

If you're a newbie, you will find that learning how to play mandolin in this tuning will be almost immediately rewarding, because it's really hard to sound bad playing in Dead Man's Tuning! The wonderful thing about open tunings, is that playing simple melodies is easy on the top two strings, and instead of being forced to learn a lot of chords, the bottom strings can "drone" along as you strum them. This is similar in the way that a bagpipe works, where one pipe plays the main melody and the other pipes act as the drone, which is the semi-chordal tone that you hear underneath the melody in bagpipe music.

This type of sound isn't confined to the world of bagpipe playing, however. There are many open tunings that are popular for the guitar as well, and you can find many famous recordings, especially in early blues music, that use open tunings to great effect. You only need to listen to most of the recordings by the early bluesman Robert Johnson, or the many people who appreciated his style such as Elmore James and Eric Clapton, to hear open tunings at work.

For most songs in the bluegrass, folk and Celtic mandolin styles Standard Tuning has been the, well….standard! And I have found that though there are a few people out there who "fiddle" around with this tuning, most players seem to stick with the typical tuning. And those who do, tend to play simply with a melody and allow the bottom strings to drone along with the melody.

When I first started playing in this style, I only had one mandolin, and I enjoyed playing in GCGC tuning. But I didn't want to retune my mandolin all the time, so I started learning how to play in different keys in the same tuning. When I switched over to DDAD tuning, I was forced to figure out how to play many different chords that work with this tuning, and it became a passionate pursuit of all that could be accomplished using this tuning. The fruit of that pursuit is what you hold in your hands.

You will find in this book several songs that I wrote for some of my students to learn this style, and several songs that are bluegrass and Celtic standards re-tabbed into this tuning. I have found in some cases, some of the songs that were originally done in other keys, when transposed into this tuning are actually quite a great deal easier to play.

Some people who are new to the mandolin may be reading this and are excited about playing, but you have yet to purchase your first mandolin, and may even be confused as to which type you should buy. So I would like to spend a couple minutes going over the types of mandolins that are available.

The mandolin is a very old instrument. A relative of the lute, the mandolin as we know it today originated in Italy in the 1700's. Like the lute the mandolin uses double strings called courses that are tuned to the same pitch. The modern mandolin has four courses of two strings, typically tuned like a violin to the pitches G D A and E. But in this book we are covering alternate tunings that are not as commonly used.

There are three common types of mandolins, and in acoustic (non electric) varieties, there are two common types. The first is the A style Mandolin.

The A stands for Appalachian, and is commonly the cheaper mandolin on the market. There are several companies that produce a playable starter mandolin for under $100 at the time of this writing, and they are perfect for the student who doesn't want to put out too much money for an instrument. My first mandolin was a Trinity River mandolin that I believe I spent about $50 on. My only complaints were that the bridge design was not the best, and it broke frequently. I had to glue it several times. I finally replaced it by creating a bridge out of a piece of Osage Orange wood, commonly called Hedge wood around where I am from. I finished the bridge off by routing out a groove and placing a piece of brass bar to form the actual bridge. I filed off the string slots and it gave the mandolin an exceptionally bright sound with a nice ring.

The other objection to this quality of mandolin was that it did not come with a neck adjustment truss rod. A truss rod is a very important aspect to any fretted instrument because if the neck warps at all, a truss rod can help bring it back into playability. However, as cheap as the mandolins are without truss rods, if it ever went out, you can just about buy a new one for the price of what it would cost to take it to a repairman to have it adjusted.

If you are a craftsman type, you might find buying a cheap mandolin and upgrading it a great deal of fun.

Not all A style mandolins are cheap however. Gibson and Martin and several other companies make very fine quality A style mandolins. Of the cheaper varieties, one of the most common complaints, though mine never had a problem in this area, is in the tuners. A lot of the lower cost mandolins seem to have problems with the tuners breaking. If you are upgrading a cheap mandolin, you might look around for some decent tuners. Keep in mind that A style mandolins use different types of tuners than F style, which require different lengths for the tuning post.

The second style of mandolin that you can buy is the F or Florentine Style mandolin. You can tell an F style mandolin very quickly because of the decorative curl near the base of neck.

There are many F style mandolins on the market for various prices, and even some that are budget models. I have found that the budget models tend to have all of the same concerns that you might find on the A styles, however the F style mandolins tend to be slightly more expensive than the A's. Both of my first mandolins were fairly inexpensive, however I did notice that the frets were a little better dressed on the F style, and the bridge was much better. Also, the F style that I bought came with a truss rod.

I have found that playing up the neck is a little easier on the F style, but after I rebuilt the bridge on the A style it was a great deal easier playing up the neck on the A as well. So really when you are choosing which style to buy, I would say go to a music store and play around with several mandolins and choose one that feels right to you.

I have noticed that when I play the F style it seems to feel more balanced in my hands, perhaps because of the addition of the curl it adds more weight to the center. But that could be just my opinion.

The third type of mandolin that you can buy is an electric mandolin. There are a few places out there where you can buy in all shapes and sizes electric mandolins. I do not own one, but I have contemplated building one. At the present all I can say about them is that I have seen two types available. Four string and Eight string varieties are out there with one and even two pickups, though I haven't seen one with three pickups yet. There are also many acoustic mandolins available with built in electronics so you can plug them in, but they have a different sound than the electric mandolins with actual electric guitar type pickups.

A final style of mandolin that is more common among classical players is the bowl-back mandolin. This mandolin usually has nylon or gut strings with a large bowl-like back made of slats of wood built over a round frame. These mandolins often have a mellow tone, much like a classical guitar.

THE ANATOMY OF THE MANDOLIN

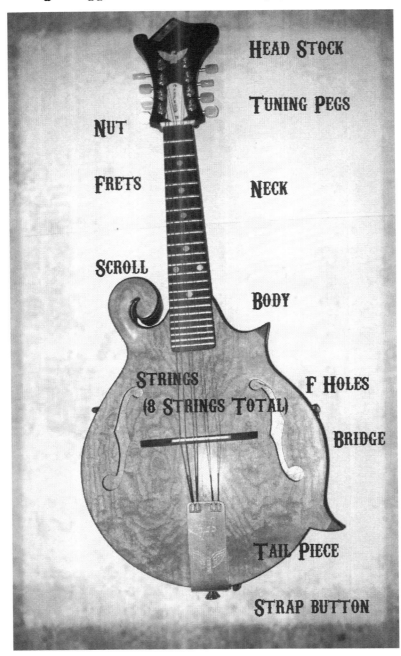

HEAD STOCK

TUNING PEGS

NUT

FRETS

NECK

SCROLL

BODY

STRINGS
(8 STRINGS TOTAL)

F HOLES

BRIDGE

TAIL PIECE

STRAP BUTTON

This mandolin is an example of fine craftsmanship, made by Larry Hopkins of Red Maple Fiddle Shop in Pekin, Indiana. Mr. Hopkins graciously allowed me to photograph several of his mandolins for use in this book. You can see more of his fine mandolins at www.redmaplechop.com.

CHAPTER 2: DEAD MAN'S TUNING HISTORY

Welcome to the fascinating tuning known as "Dead Man's" Tuning. Some call this tuning a "D cross tuning" or "Open D tuning," but regardless of what it is called, it uses the same notes of D, D an octave up, A and D an octave higher than the previous D.

Most mandolin players tune to what is known as standard tuning. Standard tuning is the same tuning that violins use, and the strings are tuned to G, D, A and E. There are many varieties of alternate tunings available for most stringed instruments, and the technical term for alternate tunings is "scordatura." Sometimes you will hear people refer to alternate tunings as cross-tunings.

I have found that Dead Man's tuning seems to be a very underrated and under used tuning, but it just happens to be my favorite tuning for the mandolin. From the information that I have gathered over the years, there are very few performers who use this tuning, perhaps because it is perceived to be a tuning which one can only play in the key of D. However, I have found that this tuning opens up a wide variety of chordal possibilities that allow the mandolinist to play in several keys that are difficult to play in using standard tuning.

As mentioned above, in Dead Man's tuning, the mandolin is tuned to D, D an octave above, A, and D another octave above. In what is called Split Dead Man's Tuning the bottom course of strings is split where the first string is tuned to D and the second string is tuned to an A. I will actually be covering three types of tunings, the final tuning in the book is a modification of Split Dead Man's Tuning, called "ADAD tuning," where the bottom course is tuned to A. So the mandolin would be tuned A, D, A, D. All three of these tunings can be used almost interchangeably with the songs that are included in this book, though each tuning gives a slightly different feel.

Dead Man's Tuning, though relatively unexplored, has been around for many years, and can be seen in songs as far back as "Bonaparte's Retreat," found in O'Neill's Music of Ireland written and published in Ireland in the late 1800's. This tuning has been compared by some to a bagpipes tuning, where one pipe is used as a melody and the other pipes are drones.

Drones are notes that sound along with the melody and never change to other notes. The drones continue to play while the tune is played over top the semi-chordal nature of the tuning.

So this tuning was used by several types of stringed instruments, such as the violin and mandolin, and a variation of the tuning was used on the banjo as well.

Other names for Dead Man's Tuning are Open D Tuning or "Bonaparte's Retreat" Tuning, or even Dee-Dad. The name Dead Man's Tuning comes from the song "Shaving A Dead Man," which was a popular old time banjo tune, also known as "Protect the Innocent," "Low D Blues," and "S.A.D.," and is still played today among folk and old time musicians. One of the most popular recordings of this song was made by Oscar Wright.

CHAPTER 3: TUNING AND TAB

Tuning the mandolin to "Split Dead Man's Tuning" is slightly different than tuning to standard tuning. Standard tuning is the same tuning that violins are tuned to: G, D, A and E, but in Dead Man's Tuning, the high strings are tuned to a D. The next course of strings down are tuned to an A, and the next course of strings are tuned down to a D an octave below the top D strings.

The bottom two strings are not tuned in the same way as the other strings. The very bottom string is tuned to D an octave below the previous D.

In a variant of Dead Man's Tuning, known as "Split Dead Man's tuning" every string is tuned as mentioned above with the exception of the bottom string. As you have seen when mandolin players say "string" what they really mean is the "course" of 2 strings that sound as one note. In Split Dead Man's Tuning you actually split the tone between the two strings of the bottom course. So the second string in the course is tuned to A an octave below the second string A, and the bottom string is tuned to a D an octave below the third string D. Once all the strings are tuned, you should have the following pattern starting at the thickest string: D/A, D an octave up, A an octave up and finally, D an octave up again.

There is a third tuning that I am relating to Dead Man's Tuning, and it is often called A-DAD tuning, rightly named because of the tuning pattern of A D A D. In this tuning the strings are tuned exactly the same way as in Split Dead Man's Tuning, but both of the bottom strings are tuned to an A instead of splitting between a D and an A.

On the next page you can see a tuning chart on how to tune to all three types of alternate tunings covered in this book.

Dead Man's Tuning Chart

Willy Minnix

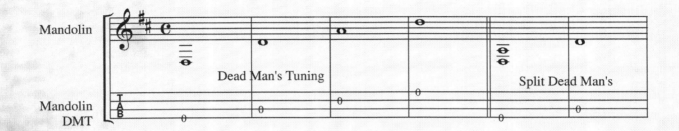

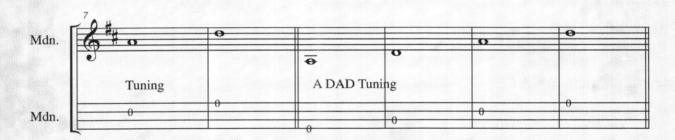

The first four measures are the notes for Dead Man's Tuning, also called D-DAD or Bonaparte's Retreat Tuning

The second four measures are in a modification of Dead Man's Tuning called Split Dead Man's Tuning. To achieve this tuning you must tune the bottom course of strings (which in standard tuning are normally tuned to an G) down to a D and an A. This will give you a drone string that is semi-chordal.

The final four measures are in a variant tuning of Dead Man's Tuning called A-DAD tuning. This tuning simply tunes the bottom course of strings to an A instead of a D. I have found that most songs played in Dead Man's Tuning can also be played in A-DAD with little impact on the playability due to the fact that the bottom string is mainly used as a drone, and very rarely plays notes.

When playing a song that uses the bottom string a lot it is better to tune to Dead Man's or A-DAD instead of Split, because sometimes there are clashing notes in Split. However, I have found that when using a pick, I can often miss the very bottom string, and pick the string tuned to A by itself on certain songs.

One of the important things that you will need to know as you proceed in this book is how to read tablature, also known as Tab. Tab is an alternate method of writing down music for stringed instruments.

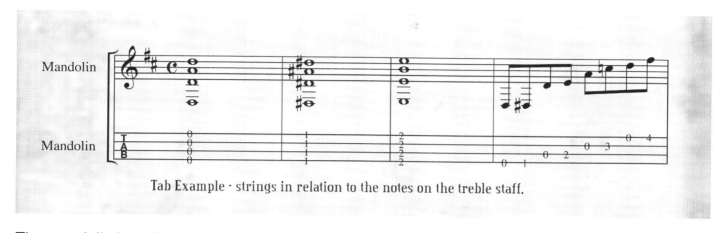

Tab Example · strings in relation to the notes on the treble staff.

The mandolin has eight strings, but when we write tablature for it we only write four strings on a line. Even in split dead man's tuning, where you technically have five pitches, I have opted only to write the tab using only four lines, since it is difficult for a beginner to single out the D from the A or vice versa when playing in Split tuning. Throughout this book Split Tuning is written just as it would be in DDAD tuning.

Each line of the tab represents a note on the mandolin. The bottom line on the tab line is the thick string on the mandolin. So in DDAD tuning that bottom line would be the D string, but in ADAD tuning it would be the A string, and in Split Dead Man's Tuning it will be a combination of a D and an A.

The second line from the bottom of the Tab line is the D, the third line up from the bottom will be the A and finally the top line will represent the highest D string.

Tablature is relatively easy. You will refer to the sheet music printed above in order to see the rhythm of the notes, and you can look at the numbers on the tab line to find out what fret you will hold as you play the strings. Sometimes you will find that instead of writing out all of the places that you strum. I have chosen to write in "light strumming throughout" or some other similar directions, so that it makes it easier to read it. I may write in a measure or two of strumming so that you can get an idea of how I play it, but I leave it up to you in a lot of places to play what you want.

One final note about tablature: you will see that in the tab there are also hammer-on's, pull-offs, bends and other markings that indicate how to play certain passages. I go into greater depth on these topics in the section on string technique.

The mandolin uses the treble clef to write the standard music on, and it is fairly easy to figure out. The lines represent notes, which are different than the tab, where the lines represent strings. The notes represented in the treble clef follow the old pattern we learned in school, Every Good, Boy, Does, Fine where the notes are E, G, B, D and F. The sharps or flats in the key signature represent the key of the piece, but for most of the songs in this book the keys of the song will either be G, which uses 1 sharp, D which uses 2 sharps, or C which uses no sharps or flats. I have tried to keep most of the songs herein in the keys of G or D, however.

Reading the rhythm of the notes is important to know how to play the melodies properly. However, you will find that with a lot of the styles represented in this book, a great deal of the melodies are "swung," which means that the beat isn't exactly always on the down beat of the song or the up beat of the song, but falls slightly behind or sometimes, though less frequently, before the main beat. Almost like the melody is limping a little bit. Don't worry; with practice you will be able to play the swung melodies with ease after a short period of time.

One of the most common problems that classically trained musicians have is learning how to swing the beat. I often tell my classically trained students to listen carefully, and if necessary, try to write out what they think they are hearing so they can analyze how the swung rhythm actually would be written if it were in standard notation. This helps them understand the way it is actually played. But once you've done that, don't be too rigid in it. The mere fact that you are swinging the rhythm means that it is loose and freeform.

Remember, the key to any of this type of music is to have fun with it. It's called "playing" music, not "working" music for a reason!

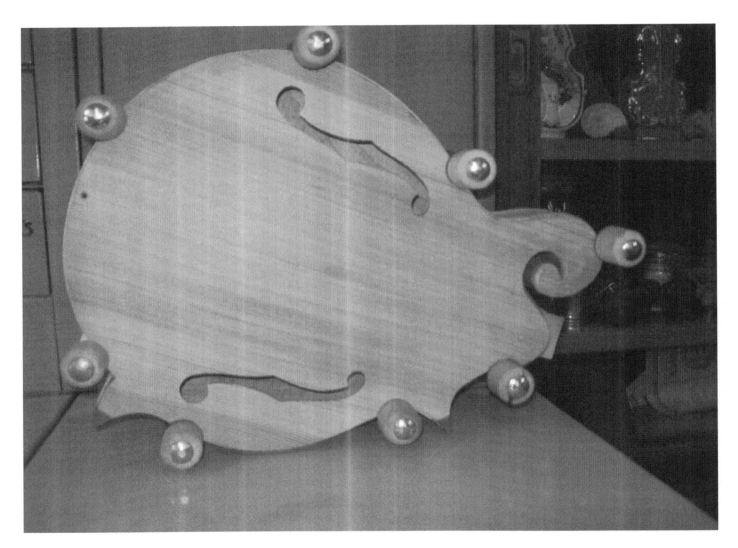

Mandolin being clamped for binding.

CHAPTER 4: DEAD MAN'S CHORDS

This section includes basic chords that you might need to play when playing in Dead Man's Tuning. The chords included here are not a comprehensive or exhaustive collection of all the possible chords you can play in this tuning, just many of the more common ones that you might find in most of the songs written or arranged in this style. As you progress in this series, you will find that I will teach you more chords with each book, so master these chords first, and then as you go along you will learn a lot more chords to add to your collection for playing in this tuning.

A chord is made up of basically three or four notes in this tuning, sometimes five depending on if you are playing in split Dead Man's tuning, where the bottom string is tuned to both a D and an A, though the notes often repeat an octave apart.

In this volume I have included the simplest way of playing some of the more common chords used in playing in the keys of D and G. You may notice that some of the chords are missing the third note of the scale. The third note is what makes a chord a chord, so technically these chords are incomplete. I have chosen to label these chords modal chords because it's not possible to tell which mode they are in, either major or minor. However, when played in the context of a song, often the implied third can be recognized, and the modal version (often the simplest way of playing the chord) works well. In later books I will show you how to play full versions of the chords, but first master what is here and then it will be easier for you to play the full version later on down the road.

Chord Theory

The technical definition of a chord is a collection of two or more notes played at the same time. A triad is a chord which has three notes played at the same time, and our ears are used to listening for triads when we play music. Most guitar and mandolin chords have three notes, with some of the notes repeated either an octave (8 notes) above or below the three main notes.

When you look at a major scale you will see that the notes that make up that scale are labeled 1 through 8, as in the illustration below:

Chord Theory

Willy Minnix

Notice these fingerings are not easy to play on mandolin

Expanded View of the Chords with notes that make up the chords

In the first part of the illustration you see each note of the scale. If you create chords using only the notes that are represented in the scale you have the next illustration with the Roman numerals labeled in them. Notice the TAB below and how it is almost impossible to play the chords using these fingerings.

This is why there are alternate fingerings for the chords on fretted instruments as opposed to the way they would be played on an instrument like the piano. The Roman numerals designate if the chord is major, using a large Roman numeral, or minor using a small roman numeral, or diminished using a small roman numeral with a degree symbol to the right.

The chords are made by using the first, third and fifth note of the particular scale for that particular note. So for instance, the first note is D, to make a chord you would stack on top of the D, kind of like drawing a snowman, the third note of the scale, which in this scale is an F#. On top of the third note you would stack the fifth note of the scale which is an A. This gives you the D major triad.

Look at the next note in the scale, the E. If you want to make a chord on the E in this key, you will have to use only notes found in this scale, but you have to use the same rules as you used for the first note D. So you must think about the E major scale, and what notes would be the third and the fifth in that scale. So for this chord, you would stack a G# on top of the E. Notice however, that there is not a G# in the Key of D. Instead, you are only given a G natural. So you must stack a G on top. What you have done in this case is flatted the third note. Finally, in the key of E you would add a B note on top of the G#, and that would give you an E major chord. But in the key of D you have used a G natural so what you get is an E with a G natural and a B on top of it, making an E minor chord.

Major chords are made by adding the 1st note + 3rd note + 5th note of the scale.

Minor chords are made by adding the 1st note + a flat 3rd note + the 5th note of the scale.

Diminished chords are made by adding the 1st note + a flat 3rd note + a flat 5th note of the scale.

So you can see that the 3rd of the chord makes a great deal of difference about whether the chord is a major chord or a minor chord. Likewise, when playing in the context of a song it is often possible to play a chord without a 3rd to infer that you are actually playing a minor or a major chord, especially if there are other instruments or voices joining the mandolin. The implied third will be heard in the ears of the listener regardless of whether the chord is there or not.

One more word about the chord fingerings, the fingerings found in the examples below are created using these notes, either an octave higher or lower, because as we just saw in the previous illustration, many of the chords cannot be played the normal way they would be written on a staff. So they need to be altered somewhat in order to produce the chords that can be used in this tuning. I believe you will find with a little bit of practice, that these chords are not that difficult to make, and are just as easy as playing two and three finger chords in standard tuning for the mandolin. Some are even easier as there are many one finger chords in this tuning.

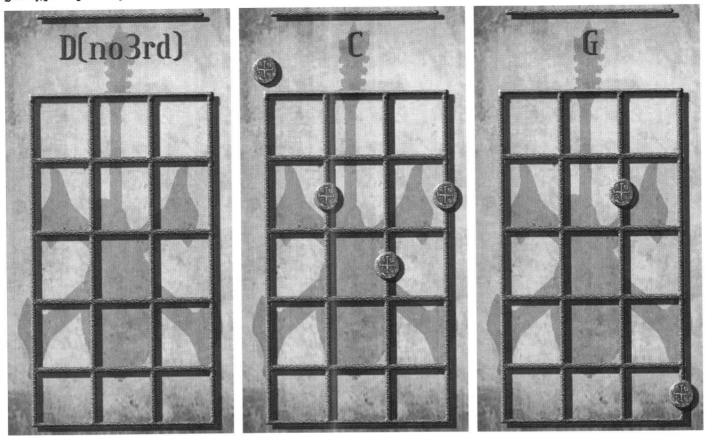

Standard and TAB notation of the chords in this book:

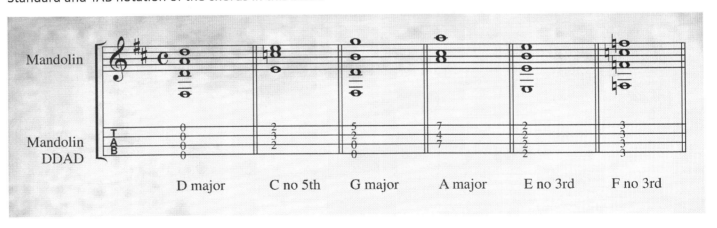

COMMON CHORD PROGRESSIONS:

Chord progressions are the backbones of songs. At their very basic, songs are made up of melodies, chords and bass lines. But many songs follow predictable patterns that have been used over and over for thousands of songs. These patterns are known as chord progressions. The chord progression is the pattern that the chords follow. Probably the most common example in popular music would be the I IV V pattern, where the I is the first chord of the scale, the IV is the fourth chord of the scale and the V is the fifth chord of the scale.

In the key of D, which is the key to which a mandolin is tuned when tuned to Dead Man's Tuning, the open strings make up a type of D chord which would be the I. The IV chord would be a G and the V chord would be an A chord. In the above diagrams you can see how to play these chords. I'm sure that if you spend a few minutes learning how to play these chords, and then strum through them, you will be able to think of several songs that you know that follow this traditional chord progression. This progression is popular in Rock, Country, Gospel, Blues and Folk music as well as several other styles of music.

Another popular chord progression is often referred to as the "Oldies Progression." It is made up by playing I, vi, IV and V as a progression. The vi chord is known as the relative minor chord, and this progression is used in many of the songs made popular in the 50's as well as rock songs from the 60's and 70's such as many doo-wop songs, and songs like "Crocodile Rock," "Stand By Me" and several other famous tunes. A variant of this progression would be I, vi, ii and V, where the ii is the minor second chord of the scale. This progression is found in the piano classic "Heart and Soul."

In the key of D the "Oldies Progression" would include the D, F#m, G and A chords. The variation would be D, F#m, Em and A.

The nice thing about chord progressions is they help you figure out and memorize how to play literally hundreds and hundreds of songs quickly and easily as soon as you know enough chords to play.

So spend some time getting to know the chords included in this volume and practice the I, IV, V and Oldies Progressions and in later volumes I will teach you more progressions and chords that will help you learn an even greater variety of songs.

Ultra-Rare 6 string Hopkins-mandolin with harmony strings added to the bottom.

CHAPTER 5: DEAD MAN'S STRING TECHNIQUE

In this chapter we are going to cover several techniques that you can use with the chords that you just learned in the last chapter, and with the songs that are included at the end of this book. In each volume I will teach you more techniques that will add to your growing repertoire, chords and other techniques that you have already learned.

HAMMER-ON

As this is the basics book, we are going to cover things that you can do with a string that every mandolin player should know. And the first thing that you will use probably every time you pick up your mandolin will be what is called the hammer-on.

Guitarists will be familiar with this technique, as it is seen often in guitar magazines and literature. The hammer-on is essentially a technique where you play a string and then slam one of your fingers down on another fret of the same string to produce a second tone without actually picking the string again. This can be accomplished either by playing the string open and then hammering down onto a fret, or by fretting a note, and then hammering with another finger on the same string.

In notation a hammer-on is notated by the use of a capital letter "H" in between the two notes involved. The first note will be the note you initially play, and the note after the "H" will be the note that you hammer onto.

The hammer can be slow or fast, but if you slow down, don't fall to the temptation of hammering too gently, because you still need to be able to make the second note sound. The other problem is that sometimes you can get in a habit of hammering to quickly and fall out of time with the rest of the music. Practice hammering until all your hammers are smooth, but clear.

PULL-OFF

The second string technique that you will use as frequently as you use a hammer-on is called a pull-off. The pull-off is basically the exact opposite of the hammer-on. Instead of hammering down onto a string, you begin by playing a fretted note, and then using the fretting finger, you pull off of the string to produce a second tone. This can either be done from pulling off of the string to an open string, or you can have another finger behind on a different fret and when you pull off that string will be sounded.

In notation a pull-off is notated by the use of a capital letter "P" in between the two notes involved. The first note will be the note you initially play, and the note after the "P" will be the note that you pull-off to.

Sometimes hammer-ons and pull-offs are played back and forth to create interesting effects. The original song included in this volume, "Dana's Tune," was written to teach how to hammer-on. On the recording of the song, found on my album "Mandolin Studies," you can hear hammering and pull-offs repeated over and over in the main motif.

The important thing to remember in both hammering and pulling off is that you don't actually pick the second note. The sound is formed by the actions of your finger on the fret, either by hammering the note, or by pulling off the string to produce another note.

DOUBLE PICKING

Another string technique that can be used is called "Double Picking." This is a very common technique used in playing the mandolin. However, it is sometimes found in classical and flamenco style guitar as well. On the mandolin it is relatively easy to accomplish this technique due to the fact that the mandolin has a double course of strings per note. If you are playing in "Split Dead Man's" tuning, then you will of course get a different effect on the bottom two strings because they are tuned differently, but in most mandolin tunings, you can double pick by playing one string on a down strum and then the other string of a course on the up strum. If you do this very quickly, you will achieve a fluttery sound that is one of the most popular string techniques heard in mandolin recordings.

One of the keys to achieving this technique is to make sure that you strum quickly and keep your pick or fingers very near the strings as you strum back and forth.

On sheet music, this technique is notated by slash marks that cut across the stem of the note that is to be played.

SLIDE

Another important technique to know in mandolin music is called the slide. The slide is used a lot in bluegrass music to slide from one note to another. Sliding is very easy. You simply fret a note, play it and then slide your finger up to a note higher up the neck, or slide down to a note lower down the neck. For example you could slide from the second fret to the fourth. It's kind of hard to slide slowly on a mandolin, but usually you'll see slides between quarter and eighth notes.

In the written music, a slide is notated by a diagonal slash going from one note to another. If the slide is going down, it will be a diagonal slash that starts at a high note and moves down to a lower note, and if it is a slide that goes up it will be just the opposite, a diagonal slash starting at a low note and ending at a high note.

VIBRATO

Vibrato is a technique more common to guitars, when the guitarist plays a fretted note and then flicks his hand back and forth as the fret is held down creating a vibrato effect. Arguably, the most famous user of this technique is B.B. King with his famous "butterfly vibrato," so called because his hand resembles a butterfly flapping its wings.

Oftentimes, double picking is used to replace this string technique in most styles of mandolin playing. While this technique is not commonly used in most popular mandolin music, it is nonetheless possible to achieve this effect in the same way that guitarist use it. It is easier when your mandolin is electrified and the volume is turned up to hear the effect.

One note of caution, you will have to develop great finger strength in order to use this technique much, but as you play your fingers will become stronger and harder and you will find that this can be one of the hidden weapons in your arsenal of techniques you can use when playing solos.

The same effect can be had by playing a fretted string, and quickly pushing the fretting hand up and down on the string where it is fretted. I find that once the technique is mastered it is actually as easy to use this technique on the mandolin as it is the guitar, it just takes getting used to having two strings under your finger instead of just one.

Vibrato is usually written on sheet music using a thick wavy line that extends for the duration of the note. If you are using vibrato on a whole note, then the wavy line would extend over the top of one measure.

BEND

The final technique, which is virtually never found in standard mandolin music, but which is found in almost all guitar literature is the bend. It is very difficult to get large bends, such as are made famous by Eric Clapton on albums like Journeyman. But it is possible to bend! This is another of those techniques that will require a great deal of hand strength.

The bend is accomplished by playing a fretted note. Then pushing up or pulling down on the string with the fretting hand, to change the pitch of the note. I find that with the top two strings I typically push up, and with the bottom two strings I typically pull down when I bend. I enjoy bending on the mandolin because it creates a distinct sound that is very different from a standard guitar bend. I find that when I play blues on the mandolin, it works out wonderfully. But a word of warning, even veteran musicians will get their fingers worn out quickly from bending too much on a mandolin. Plan on building a lot of calluses!

One of the things that helps when you bend on the mandolin is to use an amplifier. In a later volume I will teach you how to electrify your mandolin if you only have an acoustic one. This is great for you to be able to use guitar effects on your mandolin.

I had the privilege to help set up the stage for Yonder Mountain String Band one time when they played where I worked in New York, and it was really cool to see the mandolin player's set up and all of the effects he used. In the middle of the concert he played a Jimi Hendrix song on his mandolin which was amazing! So don't let yourself get boxed in to one particular style just because you are playing an instrument that has traditionally been used one way. With the use of proper effects and amplification, string bending can produce really creative and interesting sounds even on the mandolin.

A bend is notated on manuscript by the use of a curved arrow with either the word full, ½, or ¼ printed near the curved arrow. The word full shows you that you are to bend the string until the sound you hear is the same as if you were to play the note two frets up from the fret you are bending on. The ½ shows that you are to bend until you hear the note that you hear one fret up, and ¼ means that you are to bend the note until the note you hear is actually halfway between the fret you are on and the next fret up. Full bends are very difficult to achieve on the mandolin in this tuning, however, quarter and half bends are possible.

PICKING TECHNIQUES

Many mandolin players avoid finger-picking because the strings are close together. Instead they choose to focus on strumming and picking each string with a pick, also called flat picking. There are various types of picks, including smaller sized picks similar to guitar picks that have become common among mandolin players. I have always preferred finger picking, and rarely ever use a pick, except when I am playing in a venue such as a street fair where the background noise is high and the mandolin needs to be louder.

Sometimes I have opted to use finger picks when I play, though I prefer the feeling of my skin on the strings. Just because other mandolin players do not often use finger style picking on the mandolin, don't let that discourage you from trying. You might become the next Merle Travis for the mandolin!

The following examples are various styles that you can try when learning how to finger pick, and they are by no means an exhaustive list of every finger picking style, but they are some of the more common ones that you will see other string musicians using.

Finger Picking Technique

My favorite picking technique, and the one that I use more than any other technique is one made popular by blues guitarists Albert Collins and Derek Trucks. These two guitarists have been well known for picking the strings with their thumb and their first finger. I have found that I can play really fast passages with just my thumb and index finger, and on the mandolin it is easy to cover all of the strings with just two fingers. I do sometimes use finger picks. I prefer to use metal finger picks, but some of the plastic ones are very comfortable. I find I like the feel of plastic picks, but the sound of the metal ones. It is a matter of preference, but be free to experiment to find the sound and feel that appeals to you.

I really enjoy this technique because I can pick two strings at once, creating a partial chord, and then I can alternate between the thumb and the index finger when I pick out the melody. On the pauses between the melody I can pick out a lick, or I can drop my thumb down and play some bass notes on the bottom two strings. I find that a lot of the time, though not always, the index finger tends to play the top two strings, and the thumb the bottom two, but sometimes, if there is a melody that occurs mainly on the top string, I will use my thumb to cover all three of the bottom strings, so that I can create a fuller sound behind the melody.

I also find that this technique makes it very easy to switch to playing rhythm with my thumb, especially if I am wearing a thumb pick, for louder passages, or as an accompaniment to singing. As I tend to mix my picking with strumming a great deal, because I do sing a lot when I play, this type of picking appeals to me.

Banjo Patterns

I have found that a lot of mandolin players that I know are also banjo players, so it makes sense that banjo rolls could be part of a mandolin players picking arsenal.

There are a great variety of picking patterns for the banjo, though I'm only going to cover the four most basic here, and all of them are easy to play on the mandolin. The thing to keep in mind when playing banjo rolls is that they are played using three fingers. Because of this, it is useful to use fingerpicks on the thumb, first and middle fingers.

I like to play most of my rolls as triplets, and that is the way I have notated them, but they do not have to be played this way. Experiment to get the sound that works best for you.

Forward Roll

The forward roll, the way I was taught (though many banjo players call each of these rolls by different names), is made by picking on any strings using the finger pattern of thumb, index and then middle finger. As with most of these banjo rolls, it has basically a triplet feel to it. Oftentimes, the thumb alternates between the fourth and the third string each time the pattern repeats.

Backward Roll

The backward roll is exactly what it appears. It is opposite the forward roll, following the pattern middle finger, index finger and then thumb. Just like the forward roll, oftentimes the thumb will alternate between the fourth and the third string. Many times in banjo music, the player will pick the forward roll pattern for a few measures and then suddenly switch to the backward roll for a couple measures to keep the music lively.

Forward Backward Roll

The forward backward roll, also known as the forward reverse roll, starts like a forward roll, thumb, forefinger then middle, then depending on the variation of the roll, it plays the middle again, then the forefinger and then the thumb. There is another variation of it that plays the thumb, forefinger, middle, forefinger, thumb. So the two variations would look like this over a few measures, 1, 2, 3, 3, 2, 1 – 1, 2, 3, 3, 2, 1; or 1, 2, 3, 2, 1 – 2, 3, 2, 1. This second type of the forward backward roll took a little getting used to for me as the pattern seems to shift over the course of several measures.

A third variation might go Thumb, Index, Middle, Thumb, Middle, Index, Thumb, Middle. The variations are endless, which shows why there are so many differing names for a lot of the same patterns.

Reverse Roll

The last pattern is what I was taught as the reverse roll, though I have met some people who call the previous pattern and even some other patterns that I am not covering here the reverse roll. The reverse roll that I learned starts with the thumb, then plays the middle finger and then the index finger. So it would be played 1, 3, 2 – 1, 3, 2. When played over a long passage, this roll seems like it blends into and becomes basically the backward roll. You might find some books and teachers who refer to the reverse roll as: 3, 2, 1 – 3, 2, 1.

On the next page are examples and several exercises that you can practice to learn how to play this style of picking.

The author with one of the Hopkins mandolins with a sassafras top and an oak back. Notice the use of finger picks on the first finger and the thumb. This is one of my main methods of finger-picking.

Banjo Rolls on Mandolin

Willy Minnix

10 Basic Picking Patterns
For Mandolin

Example of using picking patterns along with a simple chord progression

Chapter 6: Rhythm Techniques

A lot of the songs that are standard tunes for the mandolin are based on traditional song styles. In this volume we are going to cover two traditions of song: Celtic styles, which include Irish and Scottish songs, and Bluegrass and Country styles.

One of the key elements that distinguish one style from another is the rhythm that is used in the types of songs. Most styles have a certain amount of cross over because of the influence of the older styles on the newer ones, so you will find that both Celtic music and Bluegrass music has some of the same rhythmic techniques. But you will also find that each style has some elements that are truly unique to the style.

Irish Rhythms

Reels and Jigs are not only used in fishing! They are also two types of dance tunes that are common in Irish and Scottish music, and because of the common ancestry to many Appalachian people, Bluegrass as well. Along with Reels and Jigs there are other types of dance tunes, that are also popular and in this section I am going to give you some definitions so that as we progress through this series, you will be able to tell the difference between the various kinds of musical pieces included.

Reels

Reels are primarily a 2/2 or cut time piece, relying on the use of eighth notes, accents often on the first and third beat of the measure. Often a reel has two parts with each part repeated twice. So a typical reel would have an AABB pattern. "The Maid Behind the Bar," "Drowsy Maggie," and "Cooley's Reel" are some popular reels in Irish music circles that you might run into.

Jigs

Typically a jig is a dance tune set in 6/8 time and using eighth notes primarily. However, earlier jigs sometimes have other meters as well.

Famous Jigs include, "Irish Washerwoman," and "The Kesh Jig." These two are probably the most famous jigs, however, "Father "O'Flynn," "Lark in the Morning" (a jig well suited to Dead Man's Tuning), and "Morrison's Jig" are a couple other fine examples of the genre.

When playing jigs, it is really common to use a Down Up Down Down Up Down strumming pattern.

Slip Jig

A slip jig is similar to a jig except that it commonly uses 9/8 time.

Hornpipe

Hornpipe is a dance tune traditionally associated with sailors and commonly written in 4/4 time, though examples can be found in 2/2 and even odder time signatures such as 3/2, 9/4 and 9/8 (and other types of triple time). Examples include The Sailor's Hornpipe (made popular by Popeye the Sailor), Lads of Alnwick, The Harvest Home, The Groves Hornpipe and Peacock Follows the Hen.

BLUEGRASS AND COUNTRY RHYTHMS

Bass – Strum Rhythm

This is a common rhythm used in bluegrass and country when the bass strings are picked followed by a strum of the rest of the strings. This is often heard in slower country songs, but is also used in a great deal of up beat songs as well. "Take Me Home, Country Roads" by John Denver is a decent example of this rhythm, especially in the bass guitar. Another classic example is "Hey Good Lookin'" By Hank Williams. In fact, a bunch of Hank's songs use this rhythmic technique.

Bass – Strum, Strum

This is another common rhythm that is made by picking the bass string, then strumming down on the strings, but followed immediately with an up strum. This has a bit of a triplet feel and is used more in moderate tempo and up beat tunes, though examples exist of its use in slower tunes. An example of this type of rhythmic technique can be seen in Willie Nelson's "Blue Eyes Crying In The Rain."

Down UP, Down UP

This is a typical rhythm that is pretty self explanatory, one note, however, the emphasis is typically on the first Down stroke, while the up, down, up is slightly less emphasized. There are other variations of this strum where both of the down strokes are emphasized, and any variation could be practiced to help develop good rhythmic technique. The song "Bad Day," by the band Fuel is a decent example of taking this basic strumming pattern and making it fresh and interesting.

Drone Strum

The next two rhythms are not technically rhythms in the way that the aforementioned rhythms are, but they are techniques that are used a lot on the mandolin. This first one, the Drone Strum, is a technique that imitates a bag pipe in a way. It can be used with a wide variety of strumming patterns, however, it is created by letting the bottom two strings ring out while picking out a melody on the top two strings. While this isn't technically a rhythmic technique, its use has an effect on how the rhythm of the song is conveyed, so the rhythm of the song, whatever it is, is often brought to the fore when using this technique. My version of the old Scottish ballad "Black Jack Davey" on my CD "Mandolin Studies" is an example of this technique in action.

Chop Rhythm

Chop Rhythm is a very common rhythmic technique used in many styles, but most commonly used in Bluegrass songs. It can be accomplished in two different ways. The first way is to place your fingers over the chord you are playing, after you strum the chord, immediately let up gently on your fingers to deaden the sound quickly. The sound that you are creating is an almost muted sound when you rake your pick across the strings. The second way to create this sound is to palm mute the strings by laying the fleshy part of your strumming hand against the strings near the bridge of the mandolin immediately after you strum the strings. On the guitar this technique is actually referred to as "palm muting," but I use it interchangeably with chopping often to get the same effect.

The chop technique is often used to back other instruments in band playing while the mandolin waits its turn to solo over the melody. Ricky Skaggs and other great mandolinists use this technique to great effect.

Mandolin under construction. Notice the access hole Hopkins' includes in all of his mandolins. There are two on the bottom of each mandolin, and are used to gain access to the interior of the mandolin in case they need adjustment "later down the road."

CHAPTER 7: SONGS

In this section I have included several songs that for you to start learning the basics of playing the mandolin in "Dead Man's" tuning. I have tried to pick songs that are relatively simple, yet will provide you a good foundation for other songs that will come in this series.

The first song in this volume is an original piece entitled "Corbyn's Tune." As you can see in the tab and the sheet music, it is a relatively simple tune to master. However, I have included a more complicated version on my CD "Mandolin Studies" that will show you how a simple tune can be rearranged and extended to make a more complex melody. In a later volume we will be exploring soloing techniques and how to expand your playing to a higher level, but for now master the basics, and give this tune a try.

Corbyn's Tune

Willy Minnix

Optional way of playing measure 2

Note on Recording: The recording is heavily chorused with slight delay. Second mandolin not tabbed out in this music. But it is similar to the first mandolin. Just an octave higher.

On the recording the second mandolin plays some harmonics at the 12th fret. Harmonics are made by lightly resting your finger on the string directly over the fret and plucking the string.

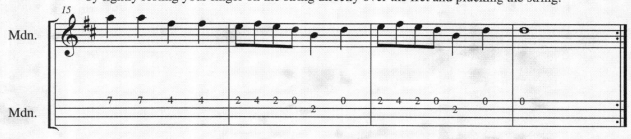

Autumn Woods

O'Neil's Music of Ireland

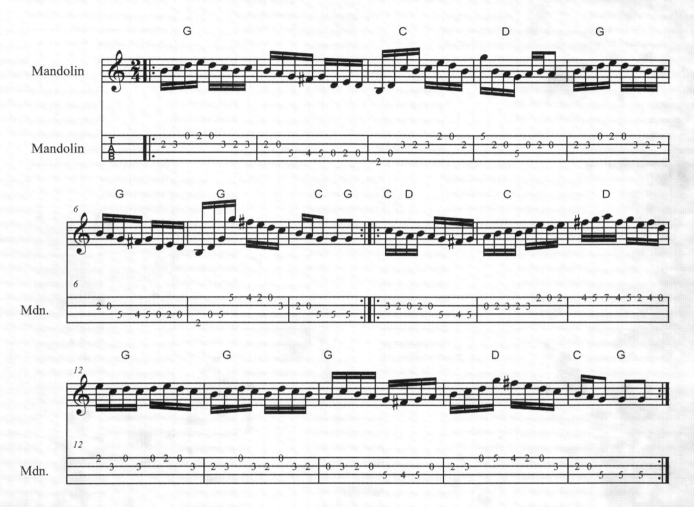

The next tune that I have included, "Autumn Woods," is a song originally found in O'Neil's Music of Ireland, a popular songbook from the late 1800's with a great deal of standard Irish dance and fiddle tunes.

Amazing Grace

John Newton arr. Willy Minnix

Amazing Grace

The second song in this collection is my interpretation of the old favorite "Amazing Grace," by John Newton. I thought this was an appropriate piece to include because not only is this a popular tune both in Celtic circles, but also in Bluegrass and Folk groups as well, but also because Newton based the original tune on an old bar tune that he knew before he was a Christian. This beloved song has been arranged both in the typical 3/4 time that is the standard way, and also in a 4/4 time to give you a chance to practice some of the rhythmic techniques that you learned in chapter 6.

Minuet in G

The third song included for your study is J.S. Bach's "Minuet in G." This beloved piano classic that most beginning piano students learn is really beautiful on the mandolin, and is perfect for the Dead Man's Tuning variant ADAD.

Minuet in G

J.S. Bach, arr. Willy Minnix

Banks of the Ohio

Traditional arr. Willy Minnix

I asked my love to take a walk,
To take a walk, just a little walk,
Down beside where the waters flow
Down by the banks of the Ohio

Chorus:

And only say that you'll be mine
And in no other's arms entwine
Down beside where the waters flow
Down by the banks of the Ohio

I held a knife against her breast
And in my arms she firmly pressed
She cried, "Oh, Willy, don't murder me,
I'm not prepared for eternity."

I started home 'twixt twelve and one
And cried, "My God, what have I done?
Killed the only woman that I loved,
Because she would not be my bride."

where the wa - ters   flow   down by the   banks   of the O hi

Banks of the Ohio is a popular bluegrass and folk tune, and I just had to include a song where the villain's name is "Willy!" In this version of the song, I have written it for two parts, one with mainly the melody line, and the other with ornamentation behind the melody. The second part should be played slightly softer than the main part. Instead of picking out the melody, the second mandolin could also strum the chords lightly behind the melody.

Trevor's Green Eyes

Willy Minnix

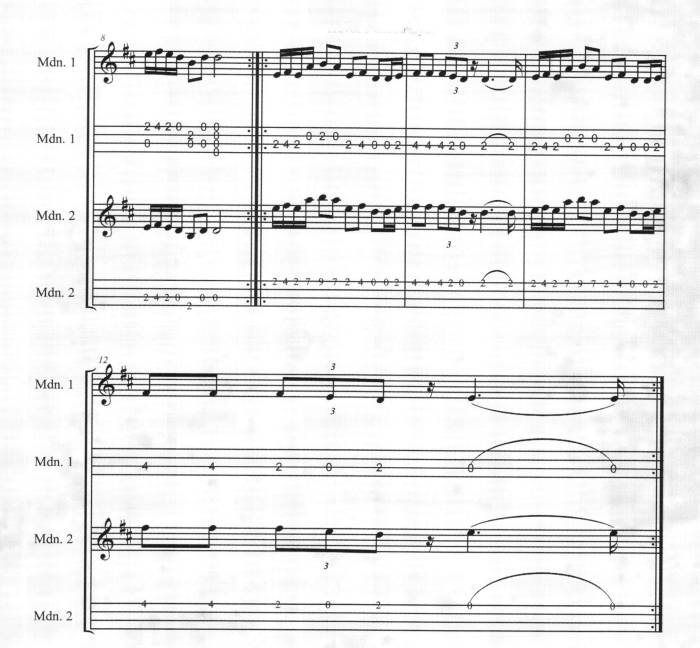

This is an original song that I wrote as a simple exercise for two mandolins.

St. James Infirmary

Trad. arr. Willy Minnix

Mandolin

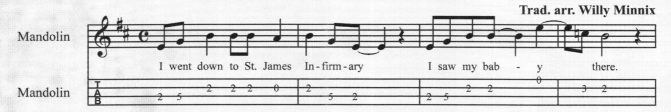

I went down to St. James In-firm-ary   I saw my bab - y   there.

Mandolin

Traditional Melody

She was on a long   whi-te tab-le   so cold so - dark and   so fair.

Mdn.

I went down - to St. James In-firm-ary   I heard my   ba-b-y cry   I was so -

Mdn.

Possible Eric Clapton
Style Intro (similar to Clapton
& Dr. John's Live VH1 Version:

New Orleans Melody (Similar to Dr. John or James Booker style)

brok-en heart-ed She's gone   some-where in -   the by   and by.

Mdn.

Other New Orleans Style Lyrics:

I went down to St. James Infirmary
I saw my baby there
She was stretched out on a long white table
With a D.O.A. sticker in her hair

When I go I want ten dollar gold piece on my eyelids
I want some loaded craps in my shoes
I want all those desperate character's around here
Play some low down dirty blues

Let her go, go on and God bless her
Wherever she may be
She could search the wide world over
And never find another man like me.

It was a cold black night last December
12 coal black hustlers on Britaneon St.
12 hustlers dressed in black leather
They was moaning and groaning outside the St. James infirmary

St. James Infirmary

Alan Lomax version from the Library of Congress recordings:
I went down to St. James Infirmary
My baby there she lay
Laid out on a cold marble table
Well I looked and turned away

What is my baby's chances
I asked old Doctor Sharp
Boy by six o'clock this evening
She'll be playing her golden harp

Let her go, let her go God bless her
Wherever she may be
She can hunt this wide world over
And never find another man like me

Sixteen coal black horses
Hitched to a rubber tired hack
Carried seven girls to the graveyard
And only brought six girls back

Now when I die bury my body
In my milk white Stetson hat
With a five dollar gold piece on my watch chain
So they'll know I died standing pat

Six poker dealers for pall bearers
Let a whore sing my funeral song
With a red hot band just beating it out
Raising hell as we roll along

Now I may be drowned in the ocean
May be killed by a cannon ball
But let me tell you buddy
A woman was the cause of it all

This classic New Orleans Jazz Blues tune is still popular all around Jazz and Blues circles. Based on "The Unfortunate Rake" tunes, it is the close relative of the cowboy tune "Streets of Laredo." I have based this version loosely on versions I heard while in New Orleans.

A Bright Evening

O'Neil's Music of Ireland

This is an old Irish tune recorded in O'Neil's Music of Ireland published in the late 1890's. As you may have noticed, "Autumn Woods" was also originally published in O'Neil's and has that distinctive Irish flair. This song is in the key of G, to give you a chance to practice other chords. Many of the songs included in this volume are in D and G.

We will eventually venture out into other keys with future volumes, but for now master these two keys, and you will do well.

The next song Dana's Tune was written to be a mandolin duet. I have played it both in split Dead Man's Tuning and also in ADAD tuning, and DDAD tuning. Either way the main melody is repeated an octave below on the second mandolin.

On the recording found on my album "Mandolin Studies," which you can find by going to www.willyminnix.com, you can hear that the main melody varies slightly as the song goes on, mainly due to the rhythmic stress on different parts of the song.

When I play live, I often segue this song into "Trevor's Green Eyes," also contained in this collection of songs. They are very similar in their melodic composition, and work well when playing them back to back.

I also use this tune as the introduction to my youtube videos that cover how to play mandolin in this style. If there are any questions that you have in this book, you can often find a video discussing the technique on one of my videos. They can be found for free by going to my website and clicking on the videos that are listed there.

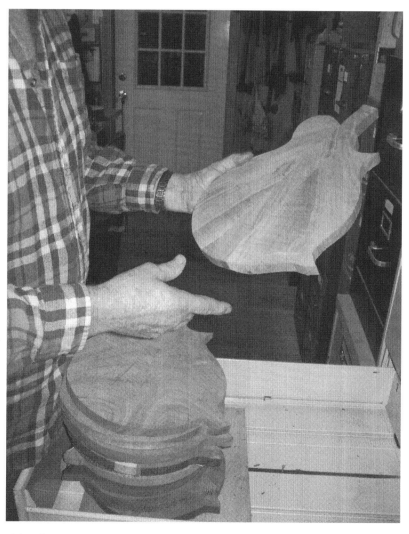

Mr. Hopkins shows a mandolin blank that will become a mandolin.

Dana's Tune

Willy Minnix

Dana's Tune

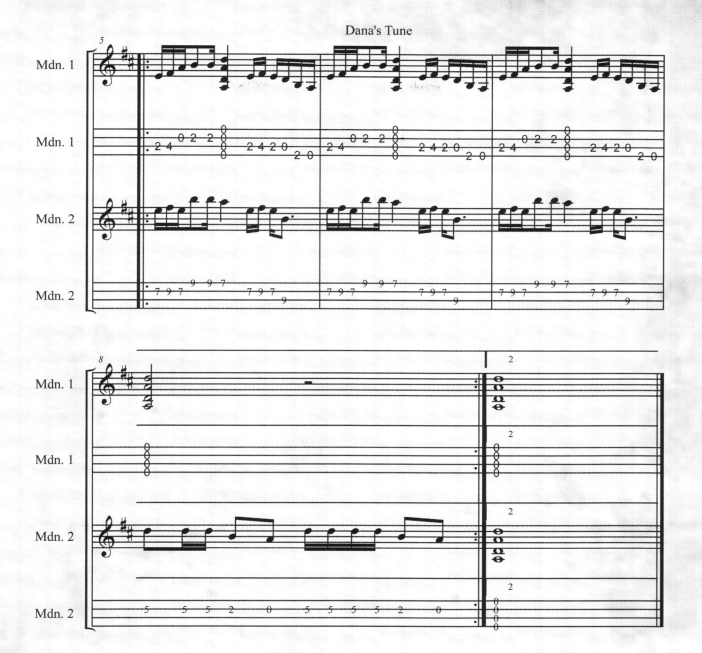

You may recognize this song as the theme song for many of my mandolin videos. I wrote this for my cousin when I was teaching her how to play mandolin. It is a duet for two mandolins, and it teaches some basic bluegrass hammering techniques that are used by fiddle and mandolin players. I wrote this as a companion piece to the song "Trevor's Green Eyes." Both songs can be played back to back by segueing from one song to the next and back again.

When Johnny Comes Marching Home

Trad. arr. Willy Minnix

Note on Key Signature: I put this in Dm but more advanced players will notice the chords are really more like open modal chords.

"When Johnny Comes Marching Home" is an old song written, as far as I can tell, during the Revolutionary War, but popularized in this form during the American Civil War. This version is written as a duet for two mandolins, one in ADAD tuning carrying the melody, and the other in Dead Man's (DDAD) carrying the rhythm and adding to the melody with heavy chordal strumming. The kids might recognize this song as "The Ants Go Marching."

Willy Minnix
Mandolin Studies

Mandolin Studies is the first companion CD that I recorded for this book series. It includes some of the songs in this book as well as several other songs covered in later books.

CHAPTER 8: LICKS AND FILLS

In this chapter I am including 16 licks and fills that I use when I play. Keep in mind that these fills can be used in any combination, and can also be included and combined with the various picking patterns that are include in chapter 5.

On the following page, the licks that are included are primarily one measure fills. In later volumes, I will be including fills that take up more than one measure, but these fills will help you in the songs you play.

Remember when using the fills, they can be used in lieu of the melody line of the song, and can also be used behind the melody line when played by another player. But primarily, these fills are perfect to be included at the end of musical phrases, or in the pauses between the melody lines.

Practice using the fills as they are written, then when you have mastered them feel free to change the fills around and create new fills out of these. Creating new fills out of the old ones is really easy to do. Just change some of the notes around and come up with fills that are unique to you and your playing style. You can change the notes, the rhythm, the sequence of the notes or just about anything else you can think of to create new fills that you can then add into the songs that you play.

As you play new fills, and as you create new fills of your own, you might consider writing them down, even if the rhythm is not perfect, so that you can keep track of the fills that you like using. You might find, years down the road, that you can go back through your journals and learn licks that you came up with before but had forgotten about. Also, as you listen to and learn from other players, feel free to write down licks that they play. By keeping track of licks, you will have a constant source of inspiration when you hit lulls in your playing that will push you onto further avenues of playing.

Check out the other volumes of Dead Man's Tuning to find new fills, licks and ways to increase your playing ability as you develop into the mandolin player you were meant to be!

Mandolin Licks and Fills

Willy Minnix

ABOUT THE AUTHOR:

Willy Minnix is a multi-instrumentalist, sound man and minister who has had the honor of working with a wide variety of bands including the Indigo Girls, Blues Traveler, Blood Sweat and Tears, the Blind Boys of Alabama and Paul Shaffer from the Late Show with David Letterman, as well as several actors including Keanu Reeves and Stanley Tucci, during his time as a sound technician. He has played music all over America with several bands and as a solo act, and teaches piano, guitar and mandolin, among other instruments.

This is his first book in a series about mandolin in the underused tuning often called "Dead Man's Tuning," "Bonaparte's Retreat Tuning," or "DeeDAD Tuning."

He lives in Indiana with his beautiful wife of 12 years and his four wonderful kids.

You can find out more about him and his music at his blog at: www.willyminnix.com

19882336R00034

Made in the USA
Lexington, KY
10 January 2013